RAISE YOUR HAND IF YOU KNOW:

ANSWERS FROM 300 TEACHERS FOR TRANSFORMING OUR PUBLIC SCHOOL SYSTEM

HAROLD BRISCOE

TATE PUBLISHING
AND ENTERPRISES, LLC

Published by Tate Publishing & Enterprises, LLC
127 E. Trade Center Terrace | Mustang, Oklahoma 73064 USA
1.888.361.9473 | www.tatepublishing.com

Tate Publishing is committed to excellence in the publishing industry. The company reflects the philosophy established by the founders, based on Psalm 68:11,

"The Lord gave the word and great was the company of those who published it."

Book design copyright © 2016 by Tate Publishing, LLC. All rights reserved.
Cover design by Albert Ceasar Compay
Interior design by Manolito Bastasa
Illustrations by Martina Crepulja and Debora Castor

Published in the United States of America

ISBN: 978-1-68254-522-5
1. Education / Educational Policy & Reform / General
2. Education / General
16.01.28

DISCLAIMER

I am a television news journalist, a high school teacher, and a parent. Some folks try to take me to task on that, but these callings uniquely prepared me to do this investigation about transforming America's underperforming and failing public schools. Of all the teachers I interviewed for this book, Teacher no. 12 sums up our predicament using one of the most colorful metaphors: "Son, we're in some pretty deep doo-doo here, but there's a way to clean it off and come out of this thing smellin' like a rose."

I believe that my investigation reveals the formula for doing this. I discovered six strategies from the interviews I did with over three hundred elementary and secondary Florida public school teachers. Now this is not another book casting aspersions or throwing bricks at the obviously mediocre to failing public school system in the United States. After all, journalists are supposed to be the watchdog for the people, not the house pet of the elites and well-connected. So this book is about fulfilling the dreams of many innovative teachers who are developing new materials and methods of instruction because they know that the status quo has not worked for decades, and Scholastic scores are proof of it.

I was asked many times to respect the privacy and anonymity of the teachers I interviewed, so I am not mentioning any of their names. Some of the reasons include the possibility of being ostracized or penalized by school or union officials. However, the purpose of my book is to enlighten you and to provide school districts all over the country with an innovative and relatively inexpensive way to improve educating their students. Enjoy!

DEDICATION

To the educators, parents, and politicians who are desperate to try new ideas to improve public school education everywhere.

My siblings: Craig, Pookie, and Connie.

Pastors Scott and Darla Young, the Harants family, and life coach, Brian Hill.

Last but not least, my parents. My dad, for putting a boot in my butt when I really needed it. My mom, for explaining to me the virtues of having a boot put in my butt in the first place. Your drive to be the best with the gifts God gave both of you inspired me to be the best with the gifts God has given me. Thanks everyone. I love you.

ACKNOWLEDGMENTS

Writing a book and getting it proofed and published is no small task. I want to thank the many people who helped me bring this book from idea to final printed page. From the researchers I cited who have done decades of studies on effective learning to the teachers in Florida, whose battle-tested mettle made this possible. I salute you all.

Ladies and gentlemen we have a crisis. We have a crisis on our hands. In many situations, our schools are perpetuating poverty....are perpetuating social failure. This calls for radical fundamental change with a huge sense of urgency. And what that takes, is a willingness to behave in ways that we have not behaved before. If we keep doing the same thing, we're going to keep getting the same results.

—Arne Duncan
United States Secretary of Education

CONTENTS

THE FEATHER

February 2000

IF THERE IS a thin line between coincidence and synchro-
nicity, between chance and purpose, I crossed it long ago
and wandered into an enchanted realm where miracles
regularly occur. It is a place where one realizes that free will
and destiny oftentimes shake hands and agree to indulge
themselves in a little rearranging of centrifugal forces,
sometimes turning lives inside out and granting the object
of their attention a massive cosmic do-over.

Remember the scenes from the movie *Forrest Gump*
where we see the feather float over the town square and
land on Forrest's shoe? Then at the end of the movie, it lifts
off from the pages of Curious George to begin its journey
again. We all get a little choked up as we figure out before
the credits roll that the feather is really a metaphor for the
interweaving of destiny and free will at various points in all
of our lives. It's there in Mama Gump's famous quote, "Life

is like a box of chocolates, you never know what you're gonna get." It's there when Jenny is singing "Blowin' in the Wind" on stage at the strip club and also present during Lieutenant Dan's stirring lament while lying legless on the hospital room floor, saying to Forrest that, "We all have a destiny." Looking back now, I see that my journey, while not nearly as cartoonish as *Forrest Gump*'s, was similar. Not to get overly philosophical, but the road traveled is always more revealing with hindsight. However, in real time, the markers of the miraculous are sometimes difficult to recognize or are downright mysterious as in *Forrest Gump*.

My story began to unfold around the end of February 2000 when I was senior television news anchor for the New York Times twenty-four-hour news channel located in Sarasota, Florida. During that time, we were reporting on the sweeping reforms in public school education being initiated by Governor Jeb Bush. For years, Florida found itself close to the bottom of the list of state-by-state public school education rankings.[1] Now all of that was changing, and it was making national headlines. I was in our Monday afternoon television news budget meeting discussing with the other reporters and staff what would be the best angle for covering these education reforms and the effect they

---

[1]   The Structure and Function of Communication in Society, Harold Lasswell, Yale Law School, 1948

would have in southwest Florida communities. As typical of news budget meetings, there was plenty of banter and debate on how to beat the other stations in the market by covering this story differently from them. My suggestion was to send a reporter "on the low-low" into the school district as a substitute teacher for a short time in order to harvest for video and sound bites. The information could come in handy if we decided to do an ongoing education series or documentary.

As I looked around the conference table, I could see heads nodding in agreement as the news staff sipped from their coffee cups and soda pop cans. Seeing the consensus, our news director said out of mere whimsy, "Okay class. What is the best way to slip a video camera into a school classroom without getting caught? *Raise your hand if you know.*"

One of our producers said, "Some shops (other television news outlets) hide it in a briefcase or mount the lens in a coat button or lapel pin. But the real trick is to have a reporter *on the inside* that has some real-life teaching experience. That way, no one will become suspicious as to what we're doing." We all agreed that would be the best way to go.

Then our news director said, "Harold, you've taught community college before. How do you feel about being our point man researching the school curriculum aspect of these education reforms?"

I nodded. Sounded good to me. "Let's run with it," I said.

The next moment, I saw hesitancy in his expression. Something came to mind that was clearly bothering him. He said, "This is going to be a very delicate operation, folks, and mining for information inside the public schools is just one part of it. Everyone's contribution will be needed for what I see as a series of package stories about education reform airing at least twice a week. Until further notice, please bring one or two story ideas about education reform to every budget meeting. This is important people!"

For my contribution, I started spending part of my shift in the station's library, looking over the school district's Web site and surfing the Web for stories about education reform in school curriculum in other states. Little did I know at the time that agreeing to this initial research would lay the groundwork for a much, much larger project to come, one that would intimately involved nearly every area of my life.

"In the same way that President Kennedy at the beginning of the 1960s said, 'At the end of the decade we're going to put a man on the moon,' and we hadn't even put a man into orbit around the Earth... I want the same focus, the same vigilance on this priority. It's a national security issue, an economic issue, a civil rights issue—it's at the very core of the future of our democracy. That is to have a human capital agenda for public schools...to have a highly effective teacher in every classroom and a highly effective principal running that school."

—Teacher no. 299, Middle School

"The next president needs to prioritize to the public the importance of the long-term economic impact of reform in our school system. If our public school system is not graduating one-third of our students, what is the long-term economic impact on our country? Teachers affect every other profession and we're the only profession that does. We have a lot of influence. If he or she can get the word out about the positive economics of revamping our schools, this will benefit everybody for a long time and it will change things in the United States."

—Teacher no. 11, Elementary School

"I consider a human soul without education like marble in the quarry, which shows none of its inherent beauties until the skill of the polisher fetches out the colors, makes the surface shine, and discovers every ornamental cloud, spot and vein that runs through the body of it."

—Joseph Addison
English Poet, Playwright, Politician

"Think about it: Every educated person is not rich, but almost every educated person has a job and a way out of poverty. So education is a fundamental solution to poverty."

—Kathleen Blanco
Fifty-fourth Governor of Louisiana

THE GENIE

March 2000

ALMOST ALL LOCAL news anchors are required by contract or by default to represent their television station at PR events sponsored by local nonprofit organizations. The colloquial phrase used inside most news shops for participating in these activities is referred to as doing a dog and pony show. The term was originally used in the United States in the late nineteenth and early twentieth centuries to refer to small traveling circuses that toured through small towns and rural areas. One of the most memorable "dog and pony shows" I was invited to participate in was the annual Celebrity Waiters Banquet. The soiree calls for three dozen of us so-called local celebrities, donning fancy aprons that display the sponsor's logo, serving dinner and drinks to a banquet hall of wealthy patrons. Money is raised for the sponsor by tips we waiters collect from our assigned tables. The big bucks of the night come when the patrons pay the master of ceremonies to have any of the waiters get on stage and publicly humiliate themselves. Things like French-kissing a donor's companion, smearing chocolate dessert all over your face or trying to play "Chopsticks" on the piano with your butt cheeks—really goofy stuff but all in the name of charity and fun. During a break in the festivities, one of the celebrity waiters, a high school principal, introduced himself to me, and we struck up a conversation. After a few minutes of small talk, he said something that caught me a little off guard because it really came from left field. He said, "Harold, I watched the story about Governor Bush's 'Just Read, Florida' program your station did earlier this week. Good job."

"Thanks," I said.

He went on. "If I went down to the beach, dug around in the sand, and found a magic lamp like Aladdin's buried there, I'd rub it and ask the genie to grant me one wish."

"Just one?" I asked. "I'd wish for three more wishes," I said.

We both laughed, but after a moment, he got serious. "I would tell the genie to turn one of our teachers into a television news reporter. That way, people would really know from an objective person of authority what's happening inside our public schools—good and bad." Then he said, "Not that the reforms aren't desperately needed, they are. But no one knows how to fix the system better than us folks who deal with kids, parents, and the teacher's union every day. Problem is nobody is asking us how, but a genie could change all that."

Okay that was creepy. I thought to myself, "Is God trying to speak to me, or is this dude just a little faded from all the alcohol we've consumed tonight?" Was this a coincidence or divine providence tapping me on the shoulder? Regardless, this sincere and unassuming man was absolutely sure he would need the superpowers of a genie to help fix the problems in public schools.

It was time to get back to work as the event's sponsor was signaling the celebrity waiters to return to their tables. However, on the way home, I couldn't stop thinking about my conversation with that school principal and how I just happen to be working on such an assignment for my television station. Coincidence? Perhaps.

On Sunday afternoons, I would always go to Siesta Key Beach for a little me time after church and family obligations. As I was walking along where the ocean hugs the shore, I reflected on the part I was to play in my station's coverage of Florida's extensive education reforms. Thoughts about the school principal invoking the power of Aladdin's genie to make these reforms happen also crossed my mind. *Why would he say such a crazy thing?* I wondered. It was the golden hour, and the sun was setting. I sat on the sugary white sand in my low-riding beach chair as the warm aqua waves of the Gulf of Mexico caressed my feet. In the distance, I could hear the rhythmic beating of drums from the circle of musicians that played on Siesta Beach every Sunday. Little by little, the soothing subtropical vibes were lulling me to nap. After the sun had slipped under the horizon, I looked down at my feet and noticed that the waves had washed a single feather over the top of my toes. I was so surprised. Was this some kind of a sign, like in *Forrest Gump*? Is there something bigger in this education reform story, or is it just another routine local television news story? What about that weird school principal guy I met? Just like him, I imagined finding a magic lamp in all this sand, rubbing it, and the genie granting me my wish. "Only one wish now," that's what the man said. I laughed. "Why a genie anyway? What's wrong with Tinker Bell or Q from *Star Trek*? How about Clarence, the angel from *It's a Wonderful Life* or, for that matter, the great and powerful Oz himself," I mused. Then I thought to myself that maybe the genie has to give the master of the magic lamp the option of three wishes because the genie knows human nature, and the lamp's owner will probably screw up the first two wishes. You can repair the damage with wish number three. Made sense. You have to be very serious and focused to only want one wish. Maybe that is what the school principal was getting at. Anyway, I was getting drowsy and starting to go off the deep end a bit, but hey, I had just watched another perfect Florida sunset at the country's number one beach, had a glass of wine, and I felt really mellow. This was neither the place nor time for serious intellectual activity. It was then that I decided to embrace my curiosity to see where my education reform reporting and the genie would take me. I had no idea how exciting things were about to get.

"I think both poles on the political spectrum are somewhat misguided but right to a certain extent. The traditional argument from folks on the Left is that schools need more money and that will fix everything. Also, we can't improve education until we fix poverty, affordable health care, and housing. The traditional argument from folks on the Right has been essentially to end education as we know it; public schools don't need tons of money anymore, and it's about more choice and more privatizing. Yes, we need to make sure our kids get their basic needs met like housing, healthcare, and good, adequate school facilities. But we can't wait for those things to happen. There is much that we can do now within the confines of the teachers' union and infrastructure to reform how public education is practiced in America today. I think that if we keep throwing money at the current system, I don't think you'll ever see much change."

—Teacher no. 50, High School

"Distance isn't a problem anymore, because now, we're competing against the whole world, and in most cases, they're doing a better job than our American schools are. One of the reasons we can't compete is because of equity—that every child is not getting the education that they deserve. We know that in twenty years, those that are considered minorities will be the majority in this country. If we look at the performance rates of those students right now, they're disproportionately underperforming on standardized tests. So we have to begin right now to make sure every child is learning, and we do so by changing the way we teach in the classroom."

—Teacher no. 160, Middle School

"What does education often do? It makes a straight-cut ditch of a free, meandering brook."

—Henry David Thoreau
American Philosopher, Abolitionist

"For every failure, there's an alternative course of action. You just have to find it. When you come to a roadblock, take a detour."

—Mary Kay Ash
Founder, Mary Kay Cosmetics

THE FORMULA

September 2000

I HAVE BEEN long-terming as a substitute teacher for a month now here at Booker High School. My students are all seniors. In the morning, I teach Speech; in the afternoon, Media Communications. The teachers and students here are friendly, though a few of them suspected I was undercover, doing a news exposé or something. That is until they learned that I had been a university and community college instructor. So far so good. I'm at school from 7:15 a.m. to 2:15 p.m. When done, I drive across town to the station to begin my anchor shift from 2:30 p.m. until 11:30 p.m. The turnaround is exhausting, but I'm trying to hang in there. Information-gathering is progressing at a snail's pace though. I still have no video yet because our engineer has been dragging his feet on making me some type of book bag or briefcase to conceal a small television camera. There is no central teacher's lounge at this school, but finding people eating together in the cafeterias or classrooms during lunch is pretty easy. One of the funnier moments I experienced here happened recently when I walked in on a group of science and social studies teachers raggin' on each other. As academicians would have it, they were telling "Yo' mama jokes" in ways only a teacher would appreciate. As an observer, I thought to myself, "Who needs drugs? These guys are high on stale-ass humor!"

Science teacher says to social studies teacher, "Why did Yo' mama's germs cross the microscope? To get to the other slide" (teachers laughing hysterically).

Social studies teacher says to science teacher, "How did Edison's invention of electricity affect society? If it weren't for him, we'd all have to watch television by candlelight" (teachers still laughing hysterically).

Science teacher says to social studies teacher, "What's the difference between ammonia and pneumonia? Ammonia comes from bottles, pneumonia comes in chests" (more hysterical laughter).

Science teacher says to social studies teacher, "Yo' mama is so illiterate she thinks claustrophobia is an unnatural fear of Santa Claus" (teachers laughing and high-fiving).

Social studies teacher says to science teacher, "Yo' mama is so stupid she thinks death was Patrick Henry's second choice" (teachers still laughing and high-fiving).

Social studies teacher says to all, "A Priest, rabbi, and a math teacher were waiting patiently on stage to be decapitated. The priest put his head in the slot, and the executioner pulled the lever; the guillotine blade went speeding down the track and stopped just a few inches above the priest's neck. The priest proclaimed that God had intervened and saved him from execution; the executioner had to agree and let him go. The mathematician had a disbelieving, puzzled look on his face.

"Next, the rabbi put his head in the slot, the executioner pulled the lever, and the blade went speeding down the track and stopped a few inches above the rabbi's neck. The executioner agreed that God had intervened again and saved the rabbi also.

"The math teacher, more troubled than ever, put his head in the slot and turned to look upward, and he noticed something that made him smile. Before the executioner could pull the lever, the math teacher said, 'Hold on there a minute, I see what the problem is! The track has a small pebble blocking the path of the blade.' He removed the pebble and announced, 'There, it should work just fine now'" (teachers whooping and hollering in near tears, laughing).

Students were peeking into the room because of all the commotion, have perplexed looks on their faces, and are befuddled about not understanding the inside punch lines to this type of humor. I must admit, it was a weird thing to watch.

Around the middle of November, the newsroom was evaluating and tweaking our Florida education reform television coverage. On the curriculum front, I reported that we would have to dedicate more resources to get video and sound bites from the school district. That could mean assigning a few more reporters to do substitute teaching at more than just one high school. I asked the staff to consider how willing we should be about expending additional effort on one specific area of education reform. Plus, the sixteen-hour days were killing me. You could tell by the expressions around the conference table that the air had been let out of the proverbial bag, and it was time for us to drop the "reporter on the inside" idea. As reality would have it, the idea was way too ambitious, and we had bitten off more than we could chew. So our television team decided that more convergence with our print-side newsroom would be a better use of our resources and story coverage. Reluctantly but with some relief, I also resigned from my teaching job at Christmas break. However, I kept all my notes because something was gnawing at me that, done right, there was still a big story here.

I kept meddling with this story idea of teachers reinventing public school education with the help of an all-powerful genie like a classic car aficionado's never-ceasing restoration of a 1957 Chevy Bel Air. I just couldn't let it go. From 2001 to 2004, I spoke off the record and on my own to a lot of teachers. My file of these conversations quickly grew during that time and would later serve as my blueprint for getting this project from the drafting board and onto the race track. The angle was different from the approach my station took in 2000. I focused on the genie; the cosmic intervention metaphor the high school principal talked to me about the night of the Celebrity Waiters fundraiser. Sadly, all his professional experience and his heart concluded that only an act of God or supernatural being could rescue our underperforming public schools. From his viewpoint, we needed a genie. It could as well have been a superhero, the Force, or space aliens. The point is, the more I listened to the teachers at various K-12 schools, the more I noticed many of their answers to solving the problems in public schools were repeating themselves, enough to be quantifiable. To explore this pattern, I decided that I had to get back inside the school system again but this time, work at as many K–12 schools as possible. The process would take a while, and it did—approximately seven years. However, the results, in my opinion, are staggering.

My semester at Booker High School showed me that in a private environment with little chance for scrutiny, ostracizing, or reprisal, my academic colleagues felt comfortable in confiding to me their ideas for a formula—a recipe, steps, strategies, or procedures. Theoretically, used in tandem, this formula would have a high probability to transform underperforming schools to higher-performing ones. After all, everyone knows there are terrific, dedicated teachers working in our public school system. I found that most of them are struggling every day to stay upright under the blows and buffeting received from tyrannical bureaucrats, clamorous parents, and unruly children. In some cases, it's their own fear, ignorance, outspoken political leanings, or their set-in-stone daily routine that's contributing to public education's failure. So with a micro tape recorder in my shirt pocket, the plan was to survey and collect data from a 10 percent sample of the nearly three thousand teachers that worked in the district at that time—around three hundred individuals.

The time was right in April 2004. My contract had come to an end at my news station, and I opted not be renewed. I was weary from the turbulence caused by an unpleasant management change at the station anyway, and if I was ever going to research and report this story, now would be the time to strike while the iron was hot, so to speak. At any rate, I was now free to move forward on my project with uninterrupted vigor. So I reapplied to the Sarasota School District and became a long-term/regular substitute. I worked in almost every K–12 school in the district, covertly interviewing hundreds of teachers along the way. By the middle of the fall 2011 school semester, I had reached my 10 percent sample goal by amassing well over three hundred interviews. While conducting those interviews, I used a single core question, based on the methodology of content analysis researcher and Yale Law School Professor Harold Lasswell.[1] My core question is what I asked every teacher in order to get them to open up, without inhibition, about what they thought needed to be done to fix our public schools. I formulated it from my conversation with that school principal who said we needed the help of a magical genie:

> If a genie, like the one in Aladdin and his magic lamp, offered to grant you only one wish for anything that could transform the education of students at your school, what would you wish for?

Now I'm not going to put up a front or pretend here. My research on this story isn't necessarily intended for full-text peer review in academic and scholarly journals. However, to the best of my ability as a researcher and a television news journalist, it is accurate. Fortunately, I do have experience in the area of content analysis of opinion poll data. I'm sure

---

[1] The Structure and Function of Communication in Society, Harold Lasswell, Yale Law School, 1948

you have seen examples of it on television, blogs, or in print. It would say something like, "Our opinion poll responses of texts, tweets, e-mails, and phone calls show 40 percent of you were against (the issue); 50 percent for it, and 10 percent of you were undecided." You get the picture. Since the 1980s, content analysis has become an increasingly important tool in the measurement of influence and success. It has also been used by futurists like Gerald Celente, John Naisbitt, and others to identify economic and cultural trends. In this age where the space between broadcast television, cable, radio, print, and Internet morph into a hybrid of content, accurately determining these medias impact on audience demographics translates into big dollars. In research of this type, content analysis is usually combined with media data (circulation, readership, clicks, number of viewers and listeners, frequency of publication, etc.). The value of this data is undisputable. As Christian Chabot, CEO of Tableau Software, said, "Data is the oil of the twenty-first century." While attending graduate school at Southern Illinois University, I used the data from focus groups to quantify in my thesis project, claims of racism or claims of good comedy writing, in episodes of the classic 1950s CBS television sitcom *The Amos 'n' Andy Show.* When I worked at Young & Rubicam Advertising-Detroit in the 1980s, my colleagues and I used similar methods for evaluating the effectiveness of audience responses to the television commercials and print ads we produced. So both my background in journalism and content research were incorporated in the fundamental analysis I did here, especially while listening to hundreds of hours of recordings and compiling the number of reoccurring "wishes" these teachers wanted the genie to grant them. You cannot imagine how stunned I was when I discovered six strategies that came out of my analysis of those interviews. I call these strategies the formula. In my opinion, it should be initiated into the operation of any underperforming public school. It consists of

1. single-sex classroom environment, whenever possible;
2. school uniform policy for all K–12 students;
3. school choice including public school tuition scholarships for all K–12 students, similar to so-called school voucher programs;
4. continuous computer-assisted reading training for all K–12 students;
5. replace teachers who are incompetent or just plain bad; and
6. corporal punishment, which may include merit/demerit-card point system, custodial work, or physical imposition (military push-ups, spanking, etc.).

"Hey, have you guys heard this one? Remember Rip Van Winkle? Okay, he wakes up in the twenty-first century after a hundred-year nap and is totally tripped out by what he sees. Men and women dash about, talking into small plastic boxes next to their ears. Young people sit at home on sofas, moving miniature athletes around on electronic screens. Older folks defy disability going about with artificial hips, knees, and little metronomes implanted in their chests. People fully recover from illnesses that used to be a death sentence like polio, meningitis, influenza, and pneumonia—just by popping a pill or getting a shot. Airports, skyscrapers, amusement parks, hospitals, and shopping malls— every place Rip goes just baffles him. But finally, when he walks into a public school classroom and looks around. He instantly recognizes exactly where he is. 'This is a school,' he declares. 'We used to have these back in 1907. Only now the blackboards are white, and the chalk is black.'"

—Teacher no. 167, High School

"Reading dogs! Reading dogs! Yeah, genie, I wish you'd grant me that! Elementary school students who have trouble reading, confidence problems, and learning disabilities can read to the dogs instead of to the class. Teachers and counselors can evaluate and select students for the program. They can stumble over words, and the dog just sits there and listens very quietly. The dogs can take a bite out of kids' fear, no pun intended, and the kids don't feel picked on."

—Teacher no. 42, Elementary School

"We spend more money per student than any other nation in the world, but the test scores of our students have fallen from near the top to near the bottom among developed nations. Our scientific and medical institutions employ so many Asians for a clear reason: they must be recruited. There are not enough qualified American students."

—Roger Ebert
Pulitzer Prize winning author and iconic
American film critic, *Chicago Sun-Times*

"You cannot fulfill the promise of the American Dream for anybody if you don't have first-rate public education…and that's a real crisis in this country."

—Cokie Roberts
Roundtable Analyst, ABC's This Week
with George Stephanopoulous

THE GOOD, THE BAD,
AND THE REALLY UGLY

December 2009

IT'S LUNCHTIME, AND as is my usual routine, I'm headed to the staff lounge to talk shop and mine for interviews. The school district is off for Christmas break beginning Monday, and everyone's in a festive mood. I can hear lots of laughter as I get to the door. After I go in and heat my black bean soup in the microwave, one of the teachers hands me a sheet of paper. She says, "Read this. It's a hoot. Sad, true, and funny all rolled into one. Like a burrito," she giggled.

I said, "Cool." She was right. I saved it because I knew I would eventually have to share it with you.

HIGH SCHOOL—1957 vs. 2009

Scenario 1:

Jack goes quail hunting before school and then pulls into the school parking lot with his shotgun in his truck's gun rack.

1957—Vice principal comes over, looks at Jack's shotgun, goes to his car, and gets his shotgun to show Jack.

2009—School goes into lockdown, FBI called, Jack hauled off to jail, and never sees his truck or gun again. Counselors called in for traumatized students and teachers.

Scenario 2:

Johnny and Mark get into a fist fight after school.

1957—Crowd gathers. Mark wins. Johnny and Mark shake hands and end up buddies.

2009—Police called and SWAT team arrives; they arrest both Johnny and Mark. They are both charged with assault and both expelled even though Johnny started it.

Scenario 3:

Jeffrey will not sit still in class, he disrupts other students.

1957—Jeffrey sent to the principal's office and given a good paddling by the principal. He then returns to class, sits still, and does not disrupt class again.

2009—Jeffrey is given a prescription for Ritalin. He becomes a zombie. He is then tested for ADHD. The family gets extra supplemental security income money from the government because Jeffrey now has a disability.

Scenario 4:

Billy is screwing around outside after being told not to and breaks a window in the next-door neighbor's car. His dad finds out and whoops Billy's butt with his belt. He makes Billy get a job after school to pay for the damage.

1957—Billy is more careful next time, grows up normal, goes to college, and becomes a successful businessman.

2009—Billy's dad is arrested for child abuse; Billy is removed from his home and placed into foster care then joins a gang. The state psychologist is told by Billy's sister that she remembers being abused herself, and their dad goes to prison. Billy's mom has an affair with the psychologist.

Scenario 5:

Sally gets a headache and takes some aspirin to school.

1957—Sally shares her aspirin with the principal out on the smoking dock.

2009—The police are called, and Sally is expelled from school for drug violations. Her car is then searched for drugs and weapons.

Scenario 6:

Pedro fails high school English.

1957 - Pedro goes to summer school, passes English and goes to college.

2009 - Pedro's cause is taken up by the state. Newspaper articles appear nationally explaining that teaching English as a requirement for graduation is racist. The ACLU files a class-

> action lawsuit against the state school system and Pedro's English teacher. English is then banned from the core curriculum. Pedro is given his diploma anyway but ends up mowing lawns for a living because he cannot speak English.

We all got a big laugh out of this in the teachers' lounge, although the facts are only slightly exaggerated. The point is we live in a society today where the mechanics of educating has to adapt quickly to change. No group knows this better than the school teachers who are battling it out every day.

Our public schools today and the people who work in them are the targets of widespread criticism. In most communities, the negativity typically comes from a local grapevine of word-of-mouth information, fertilized by media exposure on two critical issues of public education: test scores and money. The news anchor side of me always tries to be objective when looking at all of the facts of a developing story. So let's examine the good, the bad, and the really ugly. The outlook isn't entirely grim. Certainly there are school districts that are beacons of light and hope, but on average across the country, the findings are appalling.

The Good

2013 Nation's Report Card

"The Nation's Report Card informs the public about the academic achievement of elementary and secondary students in the United States. Report cards communicate the findings of the National Assessment of Educational Progress (NAEP). Since 1969, NAEP assessments have been conducted periodically in reading, mathematics, science, writing, U.S. History, civics, geography, and other subjects. The 2013 results from the Nation's Report Card shows increased scores in math, writing, reading and U.S. History for grades four, eight, and 12."[2]

Special Programs and Extracurricular Activities

If a child has any sort of special needs, including special needs for gifted children, few if any private schools in America can match what the average public school can offer access to. They include JROTC, 4-H Club, Young Entrepreneurs, International Baccalaureate programs,

---

[2]   The Nation's Report Card, National Assessment of Educational Progress (NAEP), 2011.

Vocational/Technical training, Varsity and Intramural sports, Model UN, Fellowship of Christian Athletes, AP classes, etc. There are even public schools that have a rodeo team.[1]

Public Schools are among the Safest Places Kids Can Be

Every two days in America, eleven children die from family violence, abuse, or neglect. While every child's death in any situation is a tragedy, the likelihood of violent death in schools is very low on average, making school among the safest places to be on any given day. Far less than in the workplace, where each year, almost a million people become victims of a violent crime.

Public Schools Serve the Community

Whenever hurricanes, tornadoes, floods, earthquakes, or fire threaten the community, emergency personnel assists residents with food and shelter at a local school. Where do seniors learn computer skills? Besides churches and libraries, where do people go to vote on Election Day? Where do Boys and Girl Scouts hold their meetings? Schools provide

---

[1]   What's Right with Public Schools, Anthony Odom, 2007.

an arm of support to service agencies by holding collections for clothing, food, and funds for the needy.

Guaranteed Access

Every child in America is guaranteed access to a free public education regardless of socio-economic status, gender, race, religion, desire, family connections, and mental or physical handicap. Few public school systems in the world can offer that.

The Bad

Currently in the US, 20 percent of graduating high school seniors can be classified as being functionally illiterate.[2]

Under No Child Left Behind (NCLB), many schools are meeting their annual targets for improving graduation rates. However, those states are allowed to set their own targets for improvement. More than half of those states have targets that do not make schools get better, according to a 2008 study by the Education Trust. In some states, all that's required is that schools don't do worse.[3]

---

[2] National Right to Read Foundation, 2010.
[3] Libby Quaid Associated Press, October 2008.

After testing hundreds of American, Chinese, and Japanese students in reading and math, results from a 1993 study by education researcher Harold Stevenson concluded that the Asian students consistently excelled over American students. He stated, "Clearly an achievement gap exists between American and Asian students. Part of the reason for this gap is that American students, their parents, and their teachers maintain unnecessarily low standards of performance."[4]

ABC News reported in 2009 that the cities of Cleveland, Baltimore, Atlanta, Detroit, and Chicago only graduate a slightly more than 50 percent of all their students from high school.[5]

By the fourth grade, black and Latino students on average are nearly three years behind their white and Asian counterparts. Black and Latino students are two to three times more likely to have below basic skills in reading and math. Around 50 percent of black and Latino students graduate from high school compared to 78 percent of their white-Anglo counterparts.[6]

---

[4] Stevenson, Harold, "Why Asian Students Still Outdistance Americans." Educational Leadership 50, 5 (February 1993).

[5] World News Tonight, ABC News, 2009.

[6] National Assessment of Educational Progress, 2009.

The Really Ugly

Every three years since the year 2000, the Organization for Economic Cooperation and Development administers the Program for International Student Assessment (PISA). Sixty-five countries and economies participated in PISA 2012 as of this writing, including all thirty-four OECD member countries. More than 510,000 students around the world took part in this latest survey, which compares the knowledge and skills of fifteen-year-olds in the subject areas of reading, math, and science literacy. Here are the results of how the American students were evaluated:

- The United States performed below average in mathematics and is ranked twenty-seventh. The United States ranks seventeenth in reading and twentieth in science.
- According to PISA test administrators, the United States survey results show no significant change over time since the year 2000.

In my opinion, these results are pathetic...and it gets worse:

> Just over one in four US students do not reach the PISA baseline Level 2 of mathematics proficiency— a higher-than-OECD average proportion and one that hasn't changed since 2003. At the opposite end of the proficiency scale, the US has a below-average share of top performers.

> Just over one-quarter (26%) of fifteen-year-olds in the United States do not reach the PISA baseline Level 2 of mathematics proficiency, at which level students begin to demonstrate the skills that will enable them to participate effectively and productively in life. This percentage is higher than the OECD average of 23 percent and has remained unchanged since 2003. By contrast, in Hong Kong-China, Korea, Shanghai-China, and Singapore, 10 percent of students or fewer are poor performers in mathematics.

> Punctuality and attendance at school have strong associations with performance across all countries. Some 30 percent of fifteen-year-old students in the United States reported that they had arrived late for school at least once in the two weeks prior to the PISA test, slightly below the OECD average of 35 percent, and some 20 percent of students in the United States reported that they had skipped a day of school in the previous two weeks, above the OECD average of 15 percent. Those who had skipped a class

or a day of school scored twenty-four points lower in mathematics, on average, than those who hadn't.

> While the United States spends more per student than most countries, this does not translate into better performance. A comparison of countries' actual spending per student, on average, from the age of six up to the age of fifteen also puts the United States at an advantage, since only Austria, Luxembourg, Norway, and Switzerland spend more, on average, on education per student. And yet the Slovak Republic, which spends around (USD) $5,300 per student, performs at the same level as the United States, which spends over (USD) $11,000 per student. Similarly, South Korea, the highest-performing OECD country in mathematics, spends well below the average per-student expenditure. Hong Kong/China, Finland, South Korea, and Taiwan took overall top academic honors with Germany, Ireland, Denmark, and Slovenia rounding out the bottom.[7]

---

[7] OECD (2012), Education at a Glance 2012: OECD Indicators, OECD Publishing. http://dx.doi.org/10.1787/eag-2012-en

Chart PF1.2.B: Public expenditure on primary, secondary and tertiary education, per student, 2009[1]
Expenditure per student in US$ (PPP converted)

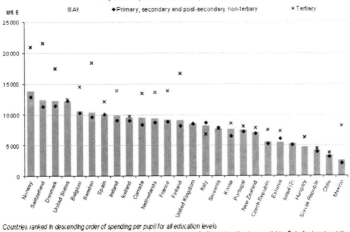

Countries ranked in descending order of spending per pupil for all education levels
Notes: Data for Hungary on primary, secondary and post-secondary non-tertiary education is unavailable. Data for Israel and the United Kingdom for tertiary education is unavailable. 1) Data refer to 2008 for Canada and 2010 for Chile. 2) see note 2 for Chart PF1.2.A
Source: OECD Education Database, 2012.

Another assessment worthy of note is the Trends in International Mathematics and Science Study administered every four years by the International Association for the Evaluation of Educational Achievement (IEA). It assesses the mathematics and science knowledge and skills of fourth and eighth graders internationally through questionnaires, tests, and extensive videotaping of classroom environments. As of this writing, the next TIMSS is scheduled for 2015. However in 2011, fifty-seven countries and other education systems administered TIMSS. Again the results show the performance of American students in comparison to their peers in other countries is barely in the top ten.[8]

---

8   The Trends in International Mathematics and Science Study, 2011.

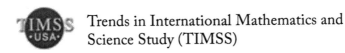 Trends in International Mathematics and
Science Study (TIMSS)

Table 2. Average mathematics scores of fourth-grade students by education system: 2011

Grade 4		
Education system	Average score	
TIMSS scale average	500	
Singapore[1]	606	Δ
Korea, Rep. of	605	Δ
Hong Kong-CHN[1]	602	Δ
Chinese Taipei-CHN	591	Δ
Japan	585	Δ
Northern Ireland-GBR[2]	562	Δ
Belgium (Flemish)-BEL	549	Δ
Finland	545	
England-GBR	542	
Russian Federation	542	
United States[1]	**541**	
Δ Average score is higher than US average score.		
Δ Average score is lower than US average score.		

Table 3. Average mathematics scores of eighth-grade students by education system: 2011

Grade 8		
Education system	Average score	
TIMSS scale average	500	
Korea, Rep. of	613	Δ
Singapore	611	Δ
Chinese Taipei-CHN	609	Δ
Hong Kong-CHN	586	Δ
Japan	570	Δ
Russian Federation	539	Δ
Israel	516	
Finland	514	
United States	**509**	

Table 4. Average science scores of 4th-grade students, by education system: 2011

Grade 4		
Education system	Average score	
TIMSS scale average	500	
Korea, Rep. of	587	Δ
Singapore	583	Δ
Finland	570	Δ
Japan	559	Δ
Russian Federation	552	Δ
Chinese Taipei-CHN	552	Δ
United States	**544**	

Table 5. Average science scores of 8th-grade students, by education system: 2011

Grade 8		
Education system	Average score	
TIMSS scale average	500	
Singapore	590	Δ
Chinese Taipei-CHN	564	Δ
Korea, Rep. of	560	Δ
Japan	558	Δ
Finland	552	Δ
Slovenia	543	Δ
Russian Federation	542	Δ
Hong Kong-CHN	535	Δ
England-GBR	533	
United States	**525**	

It even gets uglier. A report recently published by Harvard University's Program on Education Policy and Governance found that US students aren't progressing to catch up to their peers in other industrialized countries. It shows that students in Latvia, Chile, and Brazil are making gains in academics three times faster than American students while those in Portugal, Hong Kong, Germany, Poland, Liechtenstein, Slovenia, Colombia, and Lithuania are improving at twice the rate. The study's findings echo years of rankings that show foreign students outpacing their American peers academically.

Harvard researchers say that because rates of economic growth have a huge impact on the future well-being of the nation, there is a simple message: a country ignores the quality of its schools at its economic peril.

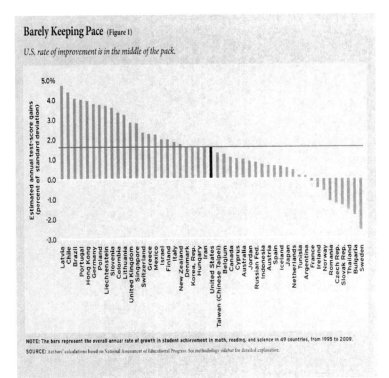

Barely Keeping Pace (Figure 1)

U.S. rate of improvement is in the middle of the pack.

NOTE: The bars represent the overall annual rate of growth in student achievement in math, reading, and science in 49 countries, from 1995 to 2009.

SOURCE: Authors' calculations based on National Assessment of Educational Progress. See methodology sidebar for detailed explanation.

Opponents would excuse the mediocre US performance by claiming that it provides a more equal education to a much more diverse population than other countries do. That argument might have made some sense fifty or seventy-five years ago, but current date suggests that this is a seriously outdated view of the world.[9]

---

[9] Huff Post Education. U.S. Students Still Lag Behind Foreign Peers, Schools Make Little Progress in Improving Achievement, September 2012

"I would ask the all-powerful public school genie to grant me the wish of having local churches adopt our schools. We could have dozens of churches and their members partnering with public schools through Bush's faith-based initiative. You know there's some federal dollars there. With all the distractions and disruptive behavior at public schools, the faiths (parochial schools) could provide mentoring, tutoring, and family support services for the kids and families with problems. Even help with employment. I'm not a Bible thumping tele-evangelist, but I'm desperate to try some new ideas. What the hell."

—Teacher no. 70, Middle School

"So I'm reading in one of the journals that schools in Japan, Philippines, and the UK are (RFID) chipping student's ID cards. This needs to be done at every school in America because we are in a state of emergency here. Lots of reasons. Sign-in and out of the main gate, to both track attendance and prevent unauthorized entrance; to mark a demerit for breaking school behavior rules, buying stuff at a school shop and canteen, library checkout, for student and teacher's attendance…shit, they're already doing it in Texas. It'll be great until some hippie's kid starts whining and files a lawsuit to fuck it up for all the other students in the district. Murphy's Law."

—Teacher no. 140, High School

"Smart businesses do not look at labor costs alone anymore. They do look at market access, transportation, telecommunications infrastructure and the education and skill level of the workforce, the development of capital and the regulatory market."

—Janet Napolitano
United States Secretary of Homeland Security

"Education is the only business that I know of, that has a monopoly. When you have a monopoly you can do whatever you want."

—Lloyd Henderson
Camden County East President, NAACP

THE EQUALIZER

January 1991

IN CHURCH TODAY, I was intently listening to our pastor use an allegory from his childhood to help illustrate a point he was making in his sermon. My feeling is that when someone who is successful in any field is secure enough within themselves to reveal their private side to help improve the quality of your own life, you should pay attention. The pastor said he wanted to show us how practical it is to use biblical principles to solve problems we encounter in our daily lives. His core text was from the Old Testament book of Proverbs 8:12 (NIV), which says, "I, wisdom, dwell with prudence, and find out the knowledge of ingenious inventions."[1] His situation—getting a beat-down in middle school nearly every day and how to avoid the same going into high school. You see, the pastor grew up in Detroit.

---

[1]   New International Version Bible Translation (Biblica), 1984.

He said he was a skinny-scrawny little kid who looked almost identical to the Steve Urkel character in the hit sitcom *Family Matters*. This caused him to almost always get picked on by some bigger boy or girl. So shortly before his freshman year in high school began, he said he studied and prayed to God the Proverbs 8:12 biblical promise of receiving wisdom and guidance for overcoming a vexing issue. He said he wanted God to show him how to spend the next four years learning at school, not surviving school. So as fall classes started, he said he felt an impression in his spirit and mind to create an alter ego he called psycho crazy man. This strategy meant that whenever he was threatened with violence at school, he would look for a huge foreign object—a brick, bat, pole, fire extinguisher, cinder block, garbage can, forty-ounce beer bottle, car bumper, anything—and try to knock his opposition out cold with it, all the while screaming and slobbering like a mad, rabid dog. It didn't take long for his "psycho crazy man" persona to develop a reputation on campus. So much so that even the most thuggish punk or gangbanger thought twice about beating him up because they knew he would go totally ballistic in a fight. The pastor called his "psycho crazy man" performance his *equalizer*. The whole church congregation was laughing hysterically as he told this story. Despite his Steve Urkel-like appearance, pastor's equalizer act nullified his opponents' perceived advantage over him.

The moral of the story is, having an "equalizer" on your side levels the playing field and increases your chances of victory over perceived insurmountable odds. In the 2013 movie version of the fable *Jack the Giant Slayer*, we see that there is no way that there can be a fair fight between people and giants. So we're introduced to a convenient device that levels the playing field: a magic crown. It's forged from ingredients including but not limited to the heart of a long-ago vanquished giant.

He who wears the crown has complete command over the giants. You whip out the crown at just the right moment and, hey, lead the giants to a conquest of all the kingdoms of Earth. That magic crown, it's an equalizer.

In 480 B.C. history tells us that in the Battle of Thermopylae, 300 Spartans, led by King Leonidas fought and nearly won against 150,000 troops of King Xerxes of the Persian Empire. Though outnumbered, their engagement with the Persians bought Greece enough time for its forces to eventually defeat the invading army in 479 B.C. thus, ushering in the world's first democracy. The Spartans brilliant use of battlefield topography, advanced weapons training, and tactical combat strategies as force multipliers are legendary. It is also required study in the techniques of warfare at many of the world's top military academies. Similar tactical brilliance was used in 1100 B.C. by the Hebrew general Gideon against 135, 00 enemy troops in the Battle of Midian. Instructed by God, Gideon's army of 300 launched a nighttime pre-attack — unheard of at the time. First, they stealthily surrounded the enemy camp. Then blew trumpets for three-minutes. Next, they held burning lanterns over their heads. At general Gideon's signal, each soldier smashes their burning lantern to the ground at the same time. Imagine how ominous these sounds and this ring of fire must have been to the Midianite army whose culture was steeped in superstition. Thousands of them panicked and turned on each another. The rest were slaughtered by Gideon's men. Both the Spartans and the Hebrews used an equalizer to lead them to incredible victories.

An equalizer is a secret weapon. It is an instrument or a formula for nullifying the enemy of illiteracy, behavioral chaos, family problems, raging hormones, and low academic test scores that plagues our students on the battlefield called the American public school system. An equalizer is also a system for turning the dynamics of the classroom learning environment upside down, inside out, and on its head. It's the formula that came from teachers. I am convinced that this formula is exactly what underachieving and failing schools districts need to use to prepare our students to become successful citizens who contribute to the greatness of United States and the world.

So after carefully cataloging, analyzing, and tallying the data from the three teachers I interviewed, these six strategies surfaced. I refer to them as the formula. Let's review them once again.

They are

1. single-sex classroom environment, whenever possible;
2. school uniform policy for all K–12 students;
3. school choice including public school tuition scholarships for all K–12 students, similar to so-called school voucher programs;
4. continuous computer-assisted reading training for all K–12 students;
5. replace teachers who are incompetent or just plain bad; and
6. corporal punishment, which may include merit/demerit-card point system, custodial work, or physical imposition (military push-ups, spanking, etc.).

Let's examine why these three hundred teachers felt so strongly that this game plan is at the core of what is critically needed to be put into action in any underperforming public school.

"My son also teaches…in Baltimore. We've talked and both agree that public schools across the country have to borrow some of the more successful strategies from the competition. For starters, working a full eight hours instead of pissing and moaning like those bitches in Chicago protesting in the streets about working more than five and a half a school day. C'mon, man! We also should be doing things like having kids go to school on Saturdays, extend the school year into part of the summer, and have universal pre-kindergarten. When you take the best stuff from these schools and districts, the things that excite and inspire kids and integrate them into your own curriculum, when you put all those ingredients together, you can get great development, great achievement, and great self-esteem from kids who do not, at this point in many cases, have an equal chance in life."

—Teacher no. 222, Middle School

"I think the Bush administration's 'No Child Left Behind' program has made some great strides. It has the best interest of kids at the heart of the law in terms of success for all students regardless of their background. It attempted to make sure that there was some rigor to the curriculum, which is a huge issue nationwide. But I think the narrow focus of how they went about it demoralizes a lot of students and teachers. I think it places too much emphasis on narrowly testing in the areas of reading, writing, and math to the detriment of arts programs, geography, social studies, which would've given us more choices to figure out how intelligent these kids actually are."

—Teacher no. 4, Elementary School

"The only really proven thing to make an economy work well is having an educated workforce. How strong the country is twenty years from now and how equitable the country is twenty years from now will be largely driven by this issue."

—Bill Gates
Founder, Microsoft

"A third of this country's students are dropping out of high school. This is the future of this nation. We are failing this generation of Americans."

—Lou Dobbs
Host, Lou Dobbs Tonight, Fox Business Network

SINGLE SEX VS. MIXED SEX: THE EVIDENCE

91 Percent of the Teachers Support Single-Gender Classes

November 2004

IT'S PLANNING TIME at the middle school I've been teaching at. Our school uses block scheduling, so every class period is about eighty-eight minutes long. Your planning period is also eighty-eight minutes. That's when you are suppose to grade tests, prepare assignments, send e-mails, have meetings, or phone parents about their kid's grades or discipline problems. My buddy, the science teacher in the classroom next door, knocks and comes in to talk and to apologize. "Hey, Mr. Briscoe, thanks for coming into my class to help break up that fight today. Just little boys trying to impress little girls and the girls using their moxie to press the little boys' buttons. Damn it, I waste ten minutes every day just to get the buggers settled down before I can begin my lesson," she said.

"Yeah, some days are better than others," I said supportively.

Then she said, "If I was a man, Mr. Briscoe, I'd give my left nut to be able to split the boys up from the girls and teach them science separately. You know there's a lot of research out there that shows that it really works."

"Really?" I said.

Then she said in exasperation, "Nothing is going to happen though. What do you expect? It's been that way and always will be like that."

A television news reporter friend of mine who lives in another state told me about a couple of identical twins she interviewed for a story. One was a crackhead, the other was totally straight—didn't smoke or drink. She asked one of the twins why she became a crackhead. She said, "What do you expect? My mother was a crackhead too." When my reporter friend asked the other twin, the non-drug user who didn't drink or even smoke cigarettes, why she was so different from her sister, she answered, "What do you expect? My mother was a crackhead." Hmmm…

What do we expect? Many people argue that one of the main reasons why America's public schools are underperforming is because of a lack of education funding. But the fact is public education spending has doubled in the last fifteen years.[1] This leaves one other argument. That is, that major flaws have developed in the mechanics of effectively educating public school students since the 1970s and academic achievement test scores bear this out. It doesn't have to be this way. So I looked at results from hundreds of scientific and education studies performed in the United States and abroad, many of them going back thirty years. Here is some evidence supporting the case for single-gender classes.

The average woman is believed to use the left hemisphere of the brain more often; this area of the brain is associated with speaking, reading, and writing. Likewise, their frontal lobe (facilitates speech, thought, and emotion) is more active.[2] Thus, girls retain and process information better with open-ended assignments that allow them to fully express themselves. They are also more likely to assume a leadership role in a single-gendered classroom setting than a coeducational one.[3] Researchers also found that females have better hearing than males, which would call for males to sit closer to the front of the classroom to

---

[1]   Associated Press, September 2003.

[2]   The Education Portal, September 2007.

[3]   M. Gurian, P. Henly, and T. Truman, *Boys and Girls Learn Differently!* (San Francisco: Jossey-Bass, 2001).

hear instruction better.[4] Also, females have higher levels of estrogen in the brain, which reduces aggressive behavior and are thought to create a calmer classroom atmosphere.[5]

According to defenders of coeducation, segregated learning facilities are inherently unequal. They say that without the presence of the opposite sex, students are denied a learning environment representative of real life. But studies on coed vs. single-sex education shows that in the single-sex environment, girls relax enough to feel comfortable exploring non-traditional subjects such as mathematics, advanced sciences, computers and technology, woodworking, and so on. They embrace sports like field hockey and soccer with gusto without worrying about appearing like tomboys. Boys lose their inhibitions about participating in choirs; they write poetry and join orchestras in single-sex settings. Research shows that boys tend to soften their competitive edge and become more collaborative in a single-sex setting. They can just be boys and not worry about what the girls might think. Girls lose their shyness and begin to take risks

---

[4] Margaret M. Ferarra, "The single gender middle school classroom: A close-up look at gender differences in learning," The Australian Association for Research in Education, http://www.aare.edu.au/05pap/fer05090.pdf.

[5] H. Grossman and S. Grossman, *Gender Issues in Education* (Massachusetts: Allyn and Bacon, 1994).

in a single-sex setting and become more competitive.[6] The data suggests that changing the gender mechanics of the traditional classroom setting can reap enormous scholastic benefits. I believe that is the reason why 91 percent of the teachers I interviewed said they favored single-sex classes because they want to try new methods that would allow them to devote more time to instruction and less time for disciplining students.[7]

---

[6] M. Gurian, P. Henly, and T. Truman, *Boys and Girls Learn Differently!* (San Francisco: Jossey-Bass, 2001).

[7] Cone-Wesson and Ramirez, 1998.

"Why are we screwing around here? Why don't we put them all in uniforms and just see what happens?"

—Teacher no. 199, High School

"I'd ask the genie to grant me one wish. My wish would be for a multisensory accelerated reading and phonics comprehension computer software program. Then I would tell the genie to make the schools teach reading twice a week and make all the kids use the software three times a week for the whole school year—no exceptions. I'm telllin' you there's a strategy that could lick this whole illiteracy problem in Florida or anywhere in America in two years or less."

—Teacher no. 1, Middle School

"Education has to be the number one civil right of the twenty-first century. We can't get it done as a partisan issue."

—Newt Gingrich,
Former Speaker of the United States
House of Representatives

"To succeed, you will soon learn, as I did, the importance of a solid foundation in the basics of education—literacy, both verbal and numerical, and communication skills."

—Alan Greenspan
Former Chairman of the United
States Federal Reserve Bank

THE POWER OF UNIFORM

96 Percent of the Teachers
Support a Strict School Uniform Policy
for All K–12 Students

April 2006

THE THIRD PERIOD bell has rung, and I'm standing outside the entrance door to my classroom to keep an eye on the students as they leave for their next class, per rules of this particular middle school. It's a safety issue here in that students will be less likely to rough-house or get into fights with so many teachers standing watch. As I'm chatting with another teacher, this tall, gangly eighth-grade boy slowly walked passed us. He's got on dark sunglasses, a bandana, loaded with bling on both hands, his grill, and around his neck. He's also wearing triple-X-sized baggy jeans in "the prison-style look"—which is hanging below your butt cheeks to totally expose your drawers or boxers. He has on a black T-shirt with huge bold words in white letters that say, "Eat Shit and Die." Most public schools across the country have a very liberal dress code. At this school, the rules say teachers can only tell students to pull their pants up and tuck their shirts. So the kids know they can pretty much wear and dress however they want. Just a few years ago, the news media picked up on a national fad where kids across the country would spend all day in school wearing their pajamas and slippers. Few, if any, were disciplined or sent home by school administrators. Well, this kid's gangster-wear appearance grabbed my colleague's attention, and she says to me, "Look at that. These kids are saggin', draggin', and laggin'—and the laggin' is their academic performance, which is reflective in the slovenly manner they're allowed to dress."

I nodded in agreement to her "saggin', draggin,' and laggin'" quip.

She then said to the boy, "Young man, pull 'em up and tuck it in."

"Shut up, bitch," he replies as he keeps walking.

Now she's mad as a hornet. "I don't have to take this crap from you," she yells. "I'm getting security. Mr. Briscoe, would you grab that young punk while I call this in?"

"With pleasure!" I said vehemently. I give chase, but by now, the saggin', draggin,' and laggin' student has rounded the corner and ducked into a classroom. Now I'm pissed off because I've lost him. Then a thought crosses my mind and shocks me like an ice-cold Gatorade shower a football coach gets after winning a big game. I stopped in my tracks and said out loud, "What the hell am I doing? This whole episode would've never happened if this kid was in a uniform and knew the school's uniform policy wasn't a joke!" I turned around and walked back to my classroom.

During my time researching this story, I discovered that middle and high schools were notorious for their lackadaisical attitude about students dressing for success. It is such a low priority. The data suggests that this is an epic mistake of monumental proportions that has perpetuated itself in American public schools for decades, teachers and principals wasting precious time nearly every day chastising students about showing too much skin, wearing clothes that are a distraction or totally inappropriate. However, some school districts have finally realized the wisdom and benefits of a no-tolerance uniform policy. An incredible 96 percent of the three hundred teachers I interviewed told me that they wished the genie would grant them a no-tolerance school uniform policy for *all* of the students in their school district. Let's look at why so many of them felt this way.

- Prevents the displaying of gang colors in schools
- Decreases violence and theft over clothing issues

- Instills discipline among students
- Reduces the need for administrators and teachers to be "clothes police" (for example, determining if a boy's shorts are too low or if a girl's cleavage is too revealing)
- Reduces distractions for students
- Instills a sense of community
- Less focus on class warfare
- Helps schools recognize people who do not belong on campus premises[1]

Here are some successful results from districts who've experimented with school uniforms. In Long Beach, California, officials found that the year after their mandatory school uniform with parental opt-out program was implemented, overall school crime decreased by 36 percent. In Seattle, Washington, which has a similar school uniform policy, they saw a decrease in truancy and tardiness. They also had no incident reports of theft in their middle schools. A principal from a Baltimore, Maryland, middle school with a voluntary uniform policy said that she noticed that students had gained a "sense of seriousness about their school work that they never had before." The

---

[1] Marian Wilde, "Do Uniforms Make School Better?" Great Schools, August 2012.

data seems to suggest that we cannot dismiss the impact of school uniforms on student morale in elementary and secondary public schools. It is no coincidence that those schools that are brave enough to sow the seeds of uniforms into their campuses are experiencing a harvest.[2]

---

[2]   Melissa Kelly, "School Uniforms, Pros and Cons," http://712 educators.about.com/cs/schoolviolence/a/uniforms_2.htm.

"Sure, more money would be nice; I mean, what moron would turn down more money for his or her school? But the dirty little secret that Ruth Cameron[3] didn't mention in her lawsuit against the Florida School Voucher program is that it wasn't about gettin' mo' money for public schools. It was really about the social humiliation of the teachers who work at *D* and *F* grade schools. C'mon, who wants the eyes of the city, state, or country looking at the crummy school where you teach? Thought of as incompetent even if you're honestly doing the best job you can, but maybe other teachers or administrators aren't as enthusiastic as you. Nobody in any business wants customers to believe that the product they produce sucks, let alone the place that they work sucks too. Choice is external pressure. That's the real skinny about vouchers, but you didn't hear that from me."

—Teacher no. 100, High School

"The Chinese, for every twenty thousand that are learning English, there are a handful of Americans learning Chinese. So if their students have a better command of English than ours do no matter what field they're in, they'll have the upper hand. I think we need to be more visionary

---

[3] Jeffrey S. Solocheck, January 6, 2006, http://www.sptimes.com/2006/01/06/State/QA__School_voucher_de.shtml.

as educators in the American school system and look at what the twenty-first century global needs are and break out of our little insular industrial age model. To be more 'future-looking' then we has been in the past."

—Teacher no. 78, High School

"If it means teenagers will stop killing each other over designer jackets, then our public schools should be able to require their students to wear school uniforms."

—Bill Clinton
Forty-second President of the United States

"Nowadays, you don't go to college, you're kinda screwed in America. And America is kinda screwed too."

—Jonathan Alter
Senior Editor, *Newsweek* Magazine

THE COMPETITION

85 Percent of the Teachers
Support "School Choice"

May 2010

IN TWELVE DAYS, school will be out for the summer. I've been long-terming all year at this particular high school teaching World history and American history courses. I found that these two classes were perfectly suited for my background as a television news journalist. I mean really, if you don't have rudimentary knowledge of geography and global affairs, television news is not the career for you. Anyway, I'm part of the Fine Arts faculty, and I'm in our second to last department team meeting before we inventory our classrooms and close down for summer vacation. Everyone is venting relief now that the Florida Comprehensive Assessment Test—the FCAT—is behind us. Unfortunately on the A–F grade scale of Florida schools, my school has been getting *D* grades for a couple of years, and that's really, really bad. The majority of us teachers here are worried that the suits in the state capitol are going swoop down on us like a barn owl on a mouse. Rumors of losing our accreditation, layoffs, and unwanted media attention have been running rampant all over campus. Our situation is reminiscent of Eastside High School in the hit 1989 movie *Lean on Me*, prior to its renaissance by Principal Joe Clark. If our test scores from the FCAT don't rise this time around, it will be a catastrophe. To add to our anxiety this year, the school has a new principal, and we all were trying to adjust to her management style while at the same time dealing with the intense pressure of getting our test scores up. Oh, by the way, our school's last principal was "reassigned" by the district because of those woefully low test scores. Our current captain is courageous, and she has a great strategy to turn things around, but the troops here are restless and fearful. This is how the conversation went in our department team meeting after we finished our classroom business. The names have been changed:

> BOB: There's going be real "school choice" next year because the district will have the choice of putting us all out to pasture if the FCAT comes back bad again.

CAROL: You know the per-oks 'n' charts (parochial and charter schools) are having another huge belly laugh at our expense again. If we get another *D* or even an *F*, I wonder how hard the state will slam us.

ALICE: Wouldn't surprise me if they tell us to do some of the things that the faiths (parochial schools) do, like uniforms and vouchers.

BOB: No, we don't need any of that voucher stuff. It just drains money from public schools and leads to segregated schools. I'm not for that.

CAROL: I know. I'm just saying if our FCAT is in the toilet again, we probably won't have any say in what the state makes us do next year. That's all I'm saying. *Vouchers* are a dirty word anyway.

TED: I don't know about that, Bob. Most Sarasota district schools are pretty good—some of the best in the state, except for ours of course. Vouchers would have no effect here. But anyone who says that they are against school vouchers because it drains resources from public schools is admitting that a lot of parents must want out of some of these failing schools because that's the only way any draining could happen.

BOB: Well, that's what I mean, not all schools everywhere, just in communities across the country where the school district is working on cylinders. I think it would drain resources from those schools, but I suppose in places like Detroit, Atlanta, DC, LA, Cleveland, and a few others I could see it working there (pause)…maybe.

ALICE: You guys hear about that school in Rhode Island that had to bring in charter teachers because they did a piss-poor job at teaching, or should I say not teaching reading? Brought them in to their own school to teach their own kids! How embarrassing is that? Hell, they could do that here. Make an example out of us too. Show us heathens how it's supposed to be done the right way, huh?

ME: You think that could happen?

TED: I don't think the state will close this school down, but if our scores are bad again…but anything could happen.

After, school recessed for the summer months, and I had some time to relax and write. I re-listened to the recording of this conversation several times. What I discovered along with the rest of my data up to this point was a noticeable trend supporting the idea of school choice (which includes a school vouchers program) among public school teachers. Many private schools and a few public schools have experimented with the concept of school choice. Research shows that schools who have experimented with it have found it to be one of the most effective ways to improve the quality of education in their communities because it separates the government financing of education from the government administration of public schools.[1] In plain English, it means that these public tuition scholarships may save many of the kids whose parents want used them to get out of underperforming and failing public schools. But what about the kids whose parents don't care enough to use public school voucher scholarships to get them out of these bad schools? Opponents of school choice vouchers say that it is better to save no children than save some children because saving no one is somehow more fair. As a reporter on the inside, this view doesn't make any sense to me, and it is not supported by 85 percent of the teachers in my investigation. Studies on the effects of school choice programs like the work done by researcher Paul Peterson of Harvard University has shown that even kids who stay in failing or underperforming public schools still benefit because of the competition voucher programs create among other public schools in a community. Dr. Peterson's study shows that underachieving public schools improve because unlike before, being lousy now has consequences. Plus, wherever

---

[1]   Paul Peterson, Harvard University, 2010.

you have a good school choice voucher program exerting competition on underachieving public schools in a district, all of the schools in that area improve. The Department of Education's own data found that students who were part of a solid school choice program graduated high school at a rate of 91 percent—that is 21 percent higher than the non-scholarship students.

In America, fifty-five million students attend our public schools. How many get tax credits or public school voucher scholarships? The answer is just one million. Only 2.3 million go to charter schools, despite good evidence that school choice really works. In April 2013, The Friedman Foundation released an in-depth analysis on the research of school choice. Twenty-three studies compared outcomes for students that had choice. Twenty-two found school choice improved student performance—twenty-two out of twenty-three. One study found no visible impact; no study found a negative impact. In our department team meeting, Bob commented that public school voucher scholarships lead to "segregated schools." However, his opinion in relation to the teachers I interviewed was in the minority. Further insight from the Friedman Foundation sheds light on this fact. Eight studies examined that issue. Seven found that school choice moved students from more racially segregated schools into less segregated ones. One found no effect; no study found that school choice increased segregation.[2] Food stamps, the GI Bill, Pell Grants, Medicare, even Section 8—they're all government voucher programs. Why can't we do the same thing with education?

Near the end of our team meeting, Alice expressed her misgivings about the idea of public schools building alliances with charter or parochial schools. Contrary to her personal feelings, a lot of educators—and parents—have recognized that what the current system has been doing for decades in traditional education has not been working for our children. Seizing an opportunity to help make a difference, the Bill & Melinda Gates Foundation sponsored the District-Charter Collaboration Compact.

In December 2010, these nine cities—Baltimore; Denver; Hartford, CN; Los Angeles; Minneapolis; Nashville, TN; New Orleans; New York City; and Rochester, NY—all announced compacts between their public school districts and public charter schools.[3] The agreements represent a bold commitment between district and charter schools to leverage and build upon each other's strengths. Districts will commit to replicating high-performing models of traditional and charter public schools while improving or closing down schools that are not serving students well.

---

[2] "A Win-Win Solution: The Empirical Evidence on School Choice," The Friedman Foundation (April 2013).

[3] Bill & Melinda Gates Foundation, December 2010.

Another goal of this partnership I found of particular note is the idea of addressing contentious and persistent tensions between district and charter schools. Issues having to do with facilities, funding, curriculum, English language learning, shared access to school data systems, and co-development methods of effective teaching. In my opinion, harnessing the brainpower of these groups in pursuit of a common mission to help all students succeed is laudable. Hopefully what is happening in these nine communities will be copied by other foundations and educators across the country. Legendary comedian and television icon Bill Cosby has a doctorate in education and has been a strong supporter of school choice. He said, "I've seen the people at four o'clock in the morning waiting, hoping that they would win a seat for their child in a better school. That is not fair. Parents deserve more choices. We have a moral and societal obligation to give our children the opportunity to succeed in school, at work, and in life. We cannot meet that obligation unless parents are empowered to select the best schools for their children."[4]

Another foundation achieving phenomenal results in education reform programs is the Wal-Mart Family Foundation's K–12 initiative. Driven by the urgent need to

---

[4] Janet Parshall Commentary. Moody Radio, February 25, 2011.

dramatically raise student achievement, particularly in low-income neighborhoods, the foundation has invested more than one billion dollars to date in initiatives that expand parental choice and equal opportunity in education—empowering parents to choose quality schools, regardless of type. Either traditional public, private, or public charter school will help spur the bold transformation of our national K–12 system of public education. The foundation focuses on three main key investments: shaping public policy, creating quality schools, and improving existing schools. All three initiatives are designed to work together and support one another. Shaping public policy serves to accelerate the creation of new good schools. Students and families in the new schools then help to shape public policy. Similarly, reformers learn from the practices in these new quality schools and can apply those findings to existing schools.[5]

---

5   Wal-Mart Family Foundation, 2011, www.waltonfamilyfoundation.org/mediacenter.

"I think the federal government with 'No Child Left Behind' and other programs should create some national standards; like a national robust assessment test so that we can make real and fair comparisons across the states. NCLB has some flaws, but it's the best piece of civil rights legislation passed in the US since 1964."

—Teacher no. 6, Elementary School

"It would be great if the genie would wave his hand and allow all public schools to compete with each other. That would open all kinds of choices and programs to students and parents that were never heard of before—things like music schools, virtual schools, sports schools. Who knows what ideas might bloom."

—Teacher no. 31, Elementary School

"Sometimes public school teachers can perceive charter schools as a threat. A threat of taking resources, of taking personnel, of taking jobs and that is not the kind of relationship we have (with The Learning Community Charter School). What the message is that needs to get out is that working together, great things can be accomplished for the children."

—Nancy Chenard
School Teacher, Veterans Memorial Elementary,
Central Falls, RI

"If I had a child in school and their school was a failing public school, and I could get a voucher to send my child to a good public school where he or she could progress, I would do that."

—Beverly Johnson
2004 New Jersey Public School Teacher of the Year

BOOT CAMP FOR THE EYES

86 Percent of the Teachers
Support Computer-Assisted Eye Training
to Increase Reading Proficiency

March 2007

I'M INTO MY fourth day of substitute teaching at one of the county's newer high schools. It's a beautiful facility. Lunch time in the teacher's lounge has been particularly rich for gathering information—lots of teachers and outstanding ideas. My work here has me serving as a teacher's assistant instead of being assigned my own class. I'm helping an algebra teacher by collecting last night's homework and passing out today's assignment. When I'm done, I sit in the back of the lecture hall and watch him do his thing. This guy isn't Mr. Personality, but he knows high school math. He's also smart enough to know that he has to keep over sixty students engaged and on task for eighty-eight minutes about a subject that's a little challenging for some. So to keep from being boring as Ben Steins' economics teacher in *Ferris Bueller's Day Off*, he turns his class into a high school version of CNBC's *Mad Money with Jim Cramer*. By using lots of cool sound-effect apps on his Macintosh and integrating humor into the way to work out algebra equations, his students are compelled to stay focused and participate. You could tell that every one of them who attempted to solve an algebra problem at the whiteboard felt like they were a contestant on *The Price is Right* with Drew Carey. The correct answer would be rewarded with the sound of football stadium cheers or boos and hisses for the wrong answer. I learned a lot from his presentation style.

He has his planning in fourth period, so as he settled into his break, I popped the question: "If a genie like the one in Aladdin and his magic lamp offered to grant you only *one wish* for anything that could transform the education of students at your school, what would that wish be?"

He thought for a moment. Then he said, "I'm retired Air Force. I'm not a career teacher. I've been doing this for six years now. Recruits in the Air Force and other branches of the military have to complete boot camp, you know—basic training. After that they can successfully serve our country in whatever capacity asked of them. Boot camp even helps to prepare a recruit for their occupational specialty." Then he said, "But in these public schools, there is no boot camp for the eyes, the muscles. The muscles in these kid's eyes are not trained. That's what is holding them back in math, science, reading, and other subjects."

I asked, "What type of boot camp are you talking about?" I wasn't sure where he was going with this.

He went further. "When I was in the Air Force, I learned that our researchers had pioneered the first breakthroughs in speed-reading in the 1940s. Refinements were made at Harvard Business School and at Reading Dynamics—the company founded by legendary education pioneer Evelyn Wood.[1] You see, Harold, we have to *train* the muscles in these children's eyes and the comprehension in their brains. As we do that, it eliminates all of the heavy-lifting and paralysis both students and teachers are experiencing across the school curriculum. As we do that, their eye movement and neuropathways will be able to process information more quickly and efficiently." He went on. "So I want the genie to make every student use a top-of-the-line computer-assisted reading software program three or more days a week to build the muscles controlling their eyes here at school. That's what we need, and that's what I want the genie to give me."

---

[1] Dr. Jay Polmar, "A Brief History of Speed Reading," www.eslteachersboard.com/cgi-bin/articles/index.pl?read=1689.

This teacher was in good company because 86 percent of his peers also said they felt that regular computer software-assisted accelerated reading should be put into the place several times a week, every week throughout a child's elementary and secondary school career. I'm not exactly sure how this could be integrated into the curriculum of a school with a large population, but that's not my call. The data tally showed that 86 percent of the teachers felt it's worth a try and can be done. After researching this idea, I believe I found out why so many of them share this opinion about having "boot camp for the eyes." Having worked in television news and public affairs as an anchor and talk show host, where quickly assimilating information is your bread and butter, me and my colleagues are keenly aware that the volume of information today's society doubles every two years. Yet in American elementary and secondary public schools, students are taught to read no faster than people one hundred years ago.

Reading is a physical skill, and it needs to be learned and practiced. Few physical skills have ever been mastered without practice. In a classroom course, you have an instructor who has traveled the road before you. His or her job is to explain the what, why, and how; to motivate, encourage, cajole, and pressure you into doing the practice and to keep working with you until you have the skill or lesson down pat. Accelerated reading computer software makes the teacher's job easier by training student's eyes to move smoothly over the text without stumbling over the words. Results are quantifiable instantly at the conclusion of that day's reading session. You do not have to wonder if your students are making progress because the software shows you how they are doing.

Most young children read either letter by letter or word by word. As an adult, this is probably not the way you read now. Just think about how your eye muscles are moving as you read this. You will probably find that you are fixing your eyes on one block of words and then moving your eyes to the next block of words and so on. You are reading blocks of words at a time, not individual words one by one. You may also notice that you do not always go from one block to the next. Sometimes you may move back to a previous block if you are unsure about something. A poor reader will become bogged down, spending a lot of time reading small blocks of words. He or she will skip back often, losing the flow and structure of the text and confusing his or her overall understanding of the subject. This irregular eye movement makes reading tiring. Poor readers tend to dislike reading because they may find it harder to concentrate and understand written information.[2] The following speed-reading/accelerated learning computer programs

---

[2] www.mindtools.com/speedrd.html.

were chosen by an independent panel of teachers who have had enough of software that claims to work, but only fails miserably at improving student's chances for academic success. The panel contains a broad range of experience from college instructors, public high school, and the private sector. They've seen the problems our students are facing and realize that the only way to handle the avalanche of reading materials they are up against is to read faster and comprehend better. I researched and evaluated several programs at various schools within my district that the teachers I talked to really liked. Also, because I am a teacher, several publishers were kind enough to send me screened copies their products. This is not an endorsement of any one, but to report how the top five are ranked:

1. 7 Speed Reading
2. ACE Reader
3. The Reader's Edge
4. EyeQ Deluxe
5. Rocket Reader[3]

---

[3]   (2015) www.speed-reading-software-review.toptenreviews.com.

"I'd like to see the Department of Education and the teacher's union mandate that all teachers get a starting salary, with a bachelor's degree, of forty thousand dollars. We should also lengthen the school day to keep high school kids in class until 4:00 p.m."

—Teacher no. 67, High School

"Most teachers will agree that some semesters, they're overwhelmed with too many students, lack of time and supplies to teach these kids the basics...much less the arts like music and literature. We know the public school system has problems. Shit, we see it in the media almost every day. But hell, what am I suppose to do? I'm just one teacher up against a tide of bullshit. Look how some of us have been trained. Many teachers' colleges stopped training us to teach phonics in 1959—1959! I didn't discover until a decade of teaching that I was doing it the wrong way. That's because we dumb down our kids with idiotic teaching methods like the anti-phonics whole-language reading method that cripples student's abilities to read. Compound that with these kids' raging hormones, their busted up family life, their fatty/sugary diet, and a barrage of pop-culture garbage. It's no wonder Johnny, Jane, Juan, Juanita, Jamal, or Jaqueesha can't read, and other countries laugh at our test scores. It's damn embarrassing."

—Teacher no. 210, Elementary School

"Too many of our children cannot read. Reading is the building block, and it must be the foundation for education reform."

—George H.W. Busch
Forty-third President of the United States

"Teachers matter. So instead of bashing them, or defending the status quo, let's offer schools a deal. Give them the resources to keep good teachers on the job, and reward the best ones. And in return, grant schools flexibility; to teach with creativity and passion; to stop teaching to the test; and to replace teachers who just aren't helping kids learn. That's a bargain worth making."

—Barak Obama
Forty-fourth President of the United States

YOU'RE FIRED!

91 Percent of the Teachers Support Replacing Their Colleagues Who Are Bad Teachers

September 2011

THE MORNING FOG was so heavy you could cut it with a knife. After exiting my car in this high school's faculty parking lot and struggling to see the entrance, I remember thinking that students were going to be late this morning. Visibility was so low that bus drivers were unable to navigate traffic routes they know like the back of their hand. It took me thirty-five minutes for a commute that normally takes fifteen. After checking in and briskly walking across campus to my assignment, I get to the classroom but cannot, for the life of me, pull the chair out from behind the desk of the teacher I was substituting for. I'm in relatively decent physical shape for a weekend warrior, so I know there is enough strength to pull an office chair out from behind a desk. But this bad boy won't budge. It's 7:28 a.m., and the principal gets on the intercom and says to teachers to excuse any tardy students because buses were coming in late due to this morning's heavy fog. "Wow, I caught a break. Must be livin' right…thank you, Lord," I said to myself. Still had to get my Active Board up, computer running, and look over this teacher's lesson plans. I hadn't done that yet because I was in a wrestling match with an office chair at seven thirty in the morning. Now I'm getting anxious, and frustration is starting to set in. Another minute goes by and finally I said, "To hell with it!" At the risk of destroying school district property I bum-rushed this chair by ripping it from whatever invisible force was holding it into place. As I did, the whole desk shook violently as if I was creating the tremors of a Category 10 earthquake. Pencils, books, papers, computer monitor, breath mints, coins and assorted knickknacks were all crashing to the floor. A few curious students were peeking in through the entrance door window, and their expression was that of "what's he doing in there?"

The commotion caught the attention of the teacher next door. This guy bursts through the adjoining classroom door yelling, "Hey what the hell's going on in here!"

To which I yelled back, "I'll tell you what the hell's going on. I can't pull the chair out from behind the desk so I can sit my butt down and get ready to teach this class, that's what the hell is going on!" Now if that wasn't weird enough, he doesn't say anything else but holds up his pointing finger, then his palm…as if to say, "Wait a minute…I got this."

He leaves and comes back thirty seconds later with scissors. He hands me a pair, introduces himself, and says, "Cut!"

"What?" I said. He points to the legs of the chair, and I notice they are tie-wrapped to the desk.

Again he says, "Cut!" We cut it loose and then he said, "You know who Paul Harvey is right?"

"What do you mean?" I said.

He replied, "You need to know the rest of the story. Me and three other teachers in this wing of the building have lunch in my room where the fridge, sink, and microwave are. You're welcome to join if you're curious" he added.

"Wouldn't miss it for all the oranges in Orlando," I said.

After my morning classes, I readied my trusty tape recorder and discretely put it inside my shirt pocket before heading to lunch. Entering the classroom where I received the invitation to join the other teachers, I was a little taken aback by the overpowering smell of cheap body spray and perfume—mixed in with the offensiveness of lingering farts. Obvious parting gifts left by the class as they headed to the cafeteria. "So gross," I said quietly to myself. Outside, the fog, which had made my morning commute so treacherous, was finally beginning to lift. You could see the dim yellow sunrays peak through the half-opened window blinds and cross the classroom to bathe my teacher friend in a warm glow as he sat at his desk, grading pop quizzes from his class. It was as if you could see his aura, kind of regal and surreal.

"Hey, Harold, glad you could join us. Be with you in a short. The kitchenette is to your right."

"Thanks," I said. As I was nuking some homemade lasagna, I could hear the other teachers come in. You could tell by the banter that this was a routine that they looked forward to.

"Hey guys, this is Harold. He's sitting in for Ned (not his real name)."

"Harold Briscoe?" one of them said. "You taught at my school middle school two years ago. I never forget a face."

Even though I didn't remember her, I played along politely. "It's good to see you again. Looks like we've come full circle," I said.

Then my scissor-welding teacher friend chimed in. "Harold got tie-wraps this morning." As if I had passed a fraternity initiation, they all laughed and patted me on the shoulder. "Ned's in another union vs. school district pissing match *again*. I mean he's not the first one, but it's funny to watch."

"Really?" I said.

"See, Ned's got tenure. The district can't touch him. He's a professional lemon dancer, taught at nine schools in eleven years. Told us he's retiring and moving to Fort Myers after his daughter graduates college next year."

"What's a lemon dancer?" I asked.

Another teacher said, "That's shop-talk slang for teachers who should be fired but can't because of the union contract. So like a bad used car, they're, well…lemons. So before school begins in the fall, administrators transfer their lemon teachers to other schools in hopes they'll either quit or at least decide to become an average teacher. It never happens though."

So I asked, "Why tie-wrap my chair to the desk. What's up with that?"

Another says, "Oh, he's just being an asshole. Ned's obsessed with the tie-wrapping thing. He does that to everybody. At every school he's ever worked. Even tie-wrapped a toilet seat to some kid's arm. He told us it was either that or he'd give the student a referral for misbehaving in his class." This was a good time for me to pose my core research question to the group.

"If a genie like the one in Aladdin and His Magic Lamp offered to grant you only *one wish* for anything that could transform the education of students at your school, what would you wish for?"

They all chimed in like the Three Stooges having an argument. "You just gotta fire these people—immediately, tenure or no tenure," said one.

"Yeah, teachers like that mess up our shine…give us average Joe and Jane's a bad rep. Everybody knows who they are. It's no secret that the lemons don't help the kids learn, which brings down test scores."

Another instructor said, "I worked at Verizon before becoming a teacher, in banking before that. If you don't produce and you're caught constantly fucking up, they shit-can you. So I'd say to the genie, 'I wish that you'd do, that voodoo that you do, by shit-canning these lemon teachers in a New York minute!'"

We all had a hearty belly laugh, but what I learned from these teachers that day is that under their breath, in the privacy of classroom walls, many admit that tenure for public school teachers should not be a perk of the profession. So I did some digging to find out why those in my data sample felt so strongly about the idea of firing bad teachers quickly was a necessary and healthy thing to do. I was amazed by this data from a study by Eric Hanushek, an economist at Stanford University. It showed that high-performing teachers cover 150 percent of the curriculum in an academic year compared to only 50 percent of their so-called low-performing/bad teacher colleagues. Therefore, high-performing teacher's students' progress three times faster than those with low-performing teachers—and they both cost the same money to the school district. But here's the shocker. The research shows that if school districts could fire the bottom 5 to 10 percent of these unproductive or so-called bad teachers and replace them with just average teachers, academic achievement in American public schools would quickly jump in ranking to a tie with Finland, who has the number one public school system on the planet.[1] I was absolutely astounded to discover this.

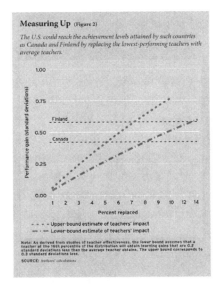

Measuring Up (Figure 2)

The U.S. could reach the achievement levels attained by such countries as Canada and Finland by replacing the lowest-performing teachers with average teachers.

---

[1]   Eric Hanushek, PhD, Stanford University, 2009.

"Teachers that I know want to help kids learn. We tolerate mediocrity, and people get paid the same, whether they are outstanding, whether they are average, or way below average. I love my (teachers) union, and they have their place, but that's the problem with having a government/civil service organization. We have a public education system, which we don't distinguish among people, and as a result of that, we don't reward excellence. Much of that has to do with teachers' union regulatory rules, which can be a nightmare. We can't weed out the bad, and until we can, we're going to have problems."

—Teacher no. 76, High School

"I wish the genie would let pay these kids in a science and math after-school work-study program. Let 'em learn and earn minimum wage or more for every hour they study. Hey, it's better than flipping burgers at McDonald's or bagging groceries. We could even give them a bonus when they make it to the end of the semester. I'd do it if I was a kid—even if my grades in math and science were okay. Only make me better, right? Couldn't hurt. I'm sure some local businesses would help. It would be good public relations for them too."

—Teacher no. 84, Middle School

"In Newark, New Jersey, one out of three thousand tenured teachers were fired last year. One out of three-thousand. That's amazing. I fire one out of six writers every year."

—Bill Maher
HBO's *Real Time with Bill Maher*

"The competition also helps. We'll all do better because of the competition."

—Peter Neilley
The Global Forecast Center
The Weather Channel

SPARE THE ROD OR SPOIL THE CHILD?

94 Percent of the Teachers Support Some Form of Corporal Punishment for Habitually Disruptive Students

May 2005

WHILE I WAS teaching speech and debate at a middle school, some of my students told me that they overheard a few of the other teachers call me the referral teacher—a well-deserved nickname that I wore as a badge of honor I might add. Instead of putting up with a student's classroom shenanigans, I gave them just one warning. They cut up again; I call security and kick the kid out of my class. I kicked a whole class out once—all twenty-five of them. Yes, it was a lot of referrals to write, but it was worth it. Middle schoolers, in general, can be particularly brazen, and as a teacher, you have to draw a line and let them know there will be consequences if they decide to cross that line. For example, after the bell rung for the beginning of second period, an eighth-grade girl in my speech and debate class decided it was time to visit with her friends instead of taking her seat. I asked her twice to please take a seat. The third time I asked her to sit down, she retorted, "All right, bitch, chill out, I'll take a seat when I'm ready." That tore it. Not only did I kick her out of my class that day, I told the principal that there will be a moratorium on my teaching if this disrespectful foul-mouthed child is allowed to set foot in my room again. It's too bad that I had to resort to threats, but I wasn't going to be like some teachers and get punked by a kid with half a brainstem and the IQ of lunch meat. Thankfully, the principal suspended her, and she was placed somewhere else when she returned to school. Later that day, as I was grading papers after school, it dawned on me that I wasn't the only teacher using up a substantial part of my instruction time dealing with behavior problems like this. I thought that there needed to be more alternatives to enforcing discipline in public school besides using harsh language, writing referrals, and making the lesson wait until security removes the disruptive element.

Another situation that stands out took place in May at the same school. The big eighth-grade trip to Universal

Studios-Orlando was days away. This meant that eighth graders had to be on their best behavior all spring semester; one slip up with a referral or suspension would take their name off the list, and they would have to remain on campus all day in study hall. These two girls in my speech and debate class were typical adolescent BFFs (best friends forever). Academically, they were getting A's and B's on almost all of their lesson assignments and were on the school's honor roll. Unfortunately, they had no inhibitions for showing their disdain for the rest of the class because they were smart and rich; and they knew the other kids knew that they were smart and rich. Their juvenile class warfare games didn't impress me any because as their instructor, the bottom line was grades. Despite the unpleasantness of their personalities, they were tops in my class. But on this particular day, ten minutes before the bell rung, they both left my class together, just bounced and booked out as I was handing back quizzes to the other students. Immediately I called security and told them to be on the lookout for Thelma and Louise (not their real names). They were soon busted. Another teacher down the hall from me allowed these girls to sit and joke around in his classroom while they ditched the last ten minutes of my class. This guy was an arrogant pinhead. "What's up with that?" I said despairingly to school security. Found out later that the kids and the teacher, Mr. Opie (not his real name) were all next-door neighbors in the same Sarasota subdivision. Guess they had some sort of student-teacher-neighborhood clique thing going on. The security resource officer said to me, "Mr. Briscoe, write up a conduct referral on them. Their immaturity is telling their pea-sized brains that they know more than the rest of us country bumpkins. Damn disrespectful these girls are…and what the hell's Mr. Opie's problem!" He went on. "You just let two kids come into your class ten minutes before the bell rings and you not say shit to them. His ass needs to be reprimanded. Probably won't happen because he's got tenure or some shit," he added.

So I wrote them up. The next day, they were so apologetic and more humble than Mother Teresa. "Please let us go to the Universal Studios trip, Mr. Briscoe. We're so sorry. We realize that we shouldn't have skipped out on the rest of class to hang out in Mr. Opie's class," they said.

My answer was still no. Later that day, Mr. Opie made it a point to come to my classroom and lobby for leniency so his girls could go on the eighth-grade trip. I might have been persuaded to change my mind had he not condescendingly told me not to be such a hard-ass with these girls because they were just kids. "Definitely no," I said.

After school was out that day, I walked across campus for a little chat with my mentor. I may be a news reporter, but I was also a teacher and a parent; I wanted to do a good job at this school. I gave her the backstory and asked her advice. She was a seasoned pro with twenty years of K–12 teaching experience in various districts and states. She told me first Mr. Opie was way out of line and should be reprimanded with a letter in his employment file. Secondly, she suggested that I give Thelma and Louise a choice: either staying in study hall the day of the eighth-grade trip or writing a fifteen-minute persuasive speech of the importance of not being an arrogant jerk by skipping class. She said, "If the knuckle heads don't want to do it, fine. Keep their butts here at school." Then she surprised me when she said, "Personally, Mr. B, me, and several of us teachers here feel that 'canoes and kids behave best when paddled from behind'. That's how you nip this behavior in the bud from jump street."

"The mentor is wise," I said half-jokingly.

But just as I got ready to walk out her door to return to my classroom, she said, "I wish we teachers had another layer of conduct control we could add to our arsenal besides referrals, different methods of corporal punishment. Make these kids do push-ups, pick up trash, use demerit cards like the faiths (parochial schools), or just paddling their butts—with permission of course—but this district will never let us do this." The sheer force of her clarity of thought was astounding. As for Thelma and Louise, they did their penance, and I allowed them to go on the trip. However, in my

opinion, paddling their little butts would have saved everybody a whole lot of time, trouble, and drama.

Ninety-four percent of the three hundred teachers
wished the genie would grant them the opportunity to
use some form of corporal punishment in their schools
with signed permission from the student's parent or
guardian. In the United States, the Supreme Court ruling
in *Ingraham v. Wright* (1977) held that school corporal
punishment does not violate the federal Constitution.[2]
Twenty-one states allow some form of corporal punishment while twenty-nine have banned the practice. Of
those states where it is used, it is only done by school
boards on a district-by-district vote. With regards to the
use of the merit/demerit system, research about its history
dates back hundreds of years to military leaders wanting
to forge loyalty and camaraderie as the soldiers learned
to defend the state. The merit/demerit system encourages
the pupil to go beyond the normal responsibility of good
citizenship and operate in an environment of kindness
and respect with their peers and instructors in the school
setting. The system acts as a hedge against negative ado-

---

[2]   430 US 651 (1977), *Ingraham et al. v. Wright et al.* No. 75-6527,
       Supreme Court of United States. Argued November 2–3,
       1976. Decided April 19, 1977, Certiorari to the United States
       Court of Appeals for the Fifth Circuit.

lescent behavior that may occur during the school day. The merit/demerit system of reward and punishment is used to encourage students to adhere to high standards of conduct, self-discipline, and personal appearance.[3]

---

[3] www.berlin-milan.org/schools/BES/GradeLevel/4th/ DISCIPLINEPOLICY2007-2008.

"The kids are not stupid, our school system is stupid. The 'there's nothing that more money can't fix' mantra is the biggest lie in America. Look at what happened in Kansas City. Billions of dollars and what did the kids get for all that money? An *F* school district and a loss of state accreditation. Son, we're in some pretty deep doo-doo, but there's a way to clean it off and come out of this thing smellin' like a rose."

—Teacher no. 12, Middle School

"Our public schools have become education prisons. When a child is very young, one to five years old, their minds are wired to learn. They are little learning machines who just adore learning. But by fourth, fifth, and sixth grades in public schools, the longer they are in there, the more it becomes a drug. They start hating learning. Why? It's because of the setting. Learning should be a joy for them throughout their K–12 career."

—Teacher no. 144, Elementary School

"We need to put everybody's hands on the table and hold people accountable. I think that's the problem. I don't think most Americans realize how bad education has fallen in our country. If there's anything Americans should be mature enough to have is a decent conversation about the education of our children."

—Rev. Al Sharpton
President, National Action Network

"This is an institution of learning, ladies and gentlemen. If you cannot control it, how can you teach? Discipline is not the enemy of enthusiasm."

—Joe Clark
Former High School Principal, Paterson, New Jersey
Lean On Me, 1989

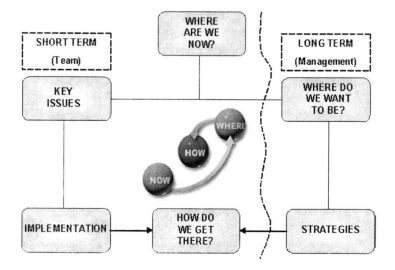

STRATEGY + DESIRE = IMPLEMENTATION

June 1992

I WAS IN Detroit at a conference by iconic peak-performance coach and best-selling author Tony Robbins. At one point during the event, Tony shared with our audience a story about how he helped a high school boy from Hawaii overcome a learning disability in a counseling session. Tony said the teen arrived at his office with a fifteen-page document from the school psychologist basically explaining why this student couldn't learn effectively. After a few minutes of reading the document and mumbling "hmm" here and there, Tony said he stopped reading. He then took one look at the young man and began ripping the report to shreds and said to the teenager, "This report is garbage!" This really changed the young man's state of my mind and perked him right up. Tony said that all the people around this young man had determined that because of dyslexia and the emotional challenges that come with it, he did not have the aptitude for learning. Robbins said that this was a foolish idea because unless something is physically wrong with your nervous system, a person can learn anything. It's just a matter of "strategy and desire." The problem was this student linked in his brain that learning in school was painful. Why? Robbins discovered that this teenager was more of a kinesthetic learner. He was more associated to his body than with pictures, and he processed things more slowly. This, along with peer pressure and family challenges, made it nearly impossible for him to focus on anything going on at school. As a result of his session with Tony, this kid's old psychological pattern was replaced with a new self-image of success. When he returned to Hawaii, he went from *D* and *F* grades to consistently making *A*, *B*, and *C* grades. The point of my using this story is to illustrate the key factor Tony Robbins talked about: strategy and desire. These teachers have told us what the formula is and are very passionate about it. However, the result of my investigation suggests that our biggest challenge is *implementation.*

Fred Hassan, former chairman and CEO of Schering-Plough, is the author of *Reinvent: A Leader's Playbook for Serial Success*. He said, "A company's cultural strategy, plus its talent, plus implementation, means success. It's the three legs of the stool."[1] Implementing the formula has the potential to create an ultimate result, a new, better destiny for our country. A destiny where "the new normal" is American students having higher test scores, a significant drop in classroom discipline problems, lower school district drop-out rates, gains in children's self-esteem, and our education system once again the envy of the world. For every positive result we get with the formula, we begin to create a direction. In other words, a cause is set in motion, there is an effect, and each effect stacks up on the one before to take that public school into a new positive direction. For every direction you're heading in, there is an ultimate destination or destiny. Urgency demands that right now, America decides what it really wants for these school children. Do we really want the best education in the world for our kids, or will we keep doing what we've been doing for decades and allow our greed, stubbornness, ignorance, fear, and political motivation to resist desperately needed new and innovate views?

So we have the game plan or *strategy* that came from my interviews with three hundred K–12 teachers. Plus, we have the *desire*; from teachers, parents, school administrators, and politicians who don't want to play the lottery anymore

---

[1]   Robert Hassan, *Reinvent: A Leader's Playbook for Serial Success* (2013).

with the future of thousands of public school students. The equation then is this: strategy + desire = implementation. So if you teach at an underperforming public school—meaning one that is ranked near or at the bottom of your school district's calculation of academic performance (a *D* or *F* on an *A–F* grading scale), there is something you can do now. Or if you are a parent or guardian of a student who may have to attend or is presently attending an under-performing public school, there is something you can also do now. That is to give copies of *Raise Your Hand If You Know*, to all the men and women who serve on your local school board of education. Do it at their next public meeting. Then, walk up to the Public Comments microphone and tell your board members that you want this book's for-mula to be used immediately transform your child's "D" or "F" public school into a successful one, beginning the Fall semester of the following year. Implore them to have mercy on the children whose destinies are in jeopardy there at that school. Ask your board members to please read this book and to make it an agenda item for discussion at their next scheduled public meeting.

In my previous chapter titled, "The Competition," I told you the story about a school I taught at that was in big trouble with state administrators because of its *D* grade academic performance rating. Fortunately, the new prin-cipal was a highly effective administrator who managed to eventually turn things around. However, she had to use the "nuclear option." I mentioned the controversial situation of Principal Joe Clark from the hit film *Lean on Me*. In the movie *Coach Carter*, the basketball coach received national attention for chaining the gymnasium doors shut and his basketball team forfeiting games because of his players' piss-poor grades. Both of these educators as well as many others across the country were/are in one of the most undesirable and difficult positions a school district employee could ever be in. That is, to have to resort to infanticide or use do-or-die tactics on teachers, staff, and students. In this reporter's opinion, these methods should have no place in public school operations. On the flipside, however, what choice does a school principal have if his/her school is so unproductive that everyone in the city and the state knows about it? How embarrassing is it to be the chief administrator or a teacher at a so-called drop-out factory? Again, in my opinion, it is a pure disgrace things have degenerated to this point in public school districts across the country. It does not have to be like this anymore.

Thankfully, these 300 teachers have given us a well-thought-out blueprint—a game-plan if you will, that can be easily implemented in any school district, to transform any struggling public school. Teachers, principals and parents need to gather their courage and insist that their local board of education follows the formula laid out in

Raise Your Hand If you Know: Answers from 300 Teachers for Transforming our Public School System. Our destiny as a nation stands at the crossroads of great public school education or mediocre public school education (at best). Do we as responsible and mature adults have the intestinal fortitude to make the right choice? As a reporter of this study, I remain cautiously optimistic.

"Boys and girls learn differently. Where was the outcry every single year when test scores came back and our kids are dropping out, can hardly read, and not going to college? Taking the pressure off boys to impress girls and off girls to impress boys out of the classroom equation will add up at test time."

—Teacher no. 263, Elementary School

"I wish we teachers had another layer of conduct control we could add to our arsenal, like the merit/demerit system used by private schools and military academies. Students with two merits or less for a month of good school behavior would be rewarded with a party or gift coupons; conversely, students with three or more demerits for bad conduct would have to listen to Mozart in study hall all day or be assigned to a clean-up team, picking up trash on the school grounds."

—Teacher no. 85, Middle School

"The paradox of education is precisely this—that as one begins to become conscious one begins to examine the society in which he is being educated."

—James A. Baldwin
American Novelist, Playwright, Poet

"The money we spend on education should follow the choice of the parents, not the choice of educrats, bureaucrats, politicians, who, unfortunately, have been manipulating this process in their own career interests, not in the interests of our young people."

—Alan Keyes
Former United States Ambassador
and Presidential Candidate

BEHOLD. I AM YOUR TEACHER!

May 2015

OPRAH WINFREY IS quoted saying, "Your true passion should feel like breathing. It should be that natural." The vast majority of teachers across the fruited plane are highly trained and motivated professionals who love their jobs and take them very seriously. But while reading over my notes and listening to my recordings, I detected an air of desperation in nearly all of them. It was a little disconcerting. In my opinion, the formula these three hundred teachers have given us is the way for our public schools to become a fertile place for students and teachers to bloom like Hibiscus flowers in a tropical garden.

I developed my television chops in public broadcasting. So as this phase of this investigation comes to a close, I hallucinate how former CBS news and public broadcasting pioneer Fred Friendly would critique it. I hope he would say that I was objective and balanced as a reporter could be under the circumstances. My personal feelings can be summed up whenever I gaze at a portrait of old socialist-realism propaganda art given to me at a faculty Christmas party a few years ago. The Russian language translation to English says, "Behold. I Am Your Teacher!" It is in a beautiful 40 × 60 oak and glass frame, the coolest gift I ever received from another teacher. Beyond the Marxist-utopian message in this picture is a reminder to all teachers to forever cherish the blind idealism and national responsibility of educating our students. The value of a life is measured by how much of it you give away to the next generation coming along behind. The headwind of today's world demands that rational, unselfish adults leverage their lives for the benefit of America's public school students.

In my assessment, there are plenty of educators out there who are innovative and want to do the right things—like the Russian teacher in my Soviet-style portrait. All children can learn when they are put into a highly effective school environment. The problem is that American teachers are forced to operate in this institutionalize bureaucracy that is driven by antiquated rules and policies that make absolutely no sense for kids or the free market. The word *education* is an interesting derivative in Latin meaning, "to bring forth from within." This is predicated on a belief that it's already there and needs help to be brought out into fruition. So if it is not coming out, then the question I have to ask is, "Who has failed who?" Of all of the in-school factors that exist today, the quality of teacher who is in front of kids every single day is what matters the most.

As an objective journalist, I am hard-pressed to offer an opinion about my reporting here. However, if I were asked, I would say that institutionalized thinking anywhere to the contrary of implementing the formula is both foolish and selfish. In the words of Bob Dylan, "The times, they are a changin'." The evidence in this report has convinced me beyond a shadow of a doubt that these three hundred teachers know better than anyone else how to reinvent our public school system. We need to bring the pendulum back and get rid of the fragmentation—get all the education participants on the same page and thinking how to better serve these students. Implementing the formula is the way to do that. It will affect our kid's idea of who they are and what they are capable of, and as that happens, it will take them in a whole new direction and, ultimately, a different destiny. Our country will reap the rewards economically, in national security, and in a newly restored position of respect and admiration around the world.

This is absolutely a battle of courage and of will. We have the ideas, we have the examples, and we have the success stories. What we have lacked is the courage to child by child, district by district, take on these tough intractable problems and fundamentally challenge the status quo. I have this huge sense of optimism about what we can accomplish.

—Arne Duncan
United States Secretary of Education

ABOUT THE AUTHOR

HAROLD BRISCOE IS a television host/news anchor, school teacher, and author. His body of work includes television commercials, theater acting, corporate training videos, and lecturing in both American and world history courses.

Reared in Kansas City, Missouri, Harold got his start in broadcasting in 1985 after getting a master's degree in broadcasting from Southern Illinois University-Carbondale. Starting in the business as a host of his own public television show *The Professionals*, he's won numerous awards, including Addy Awards (1992), National Bar Association Television Award of Merit (1992), Angel Awards (1991 and 1992), and two Emmy Award Nominations (1991 and 1992) and voted "Best Local Television News Anchor" by readers of *The Weekly Planet* newspaper, 2002.

If it has anything to do with television or entertainment, Harold has truly earned the right to say, "Been there, done that!" With more than twenty years of on-camera experience, he's moved quickly through the ranks of local television markets to become one of the most versatile national talents in the industry. With his Midwestern charm, candor, and smooth delivery, Harold is a multifaceted performer just coming into his stride. When not working, he spends his time cooking, skydiving, and training his German Shepherds.

CPSIA information can be obtained at www.ICGtesting.com
Printed in the USA
LVOW10s0454310816

502538LV00014B/87/P

9 781682 545225